Vehicles On The Move

Monster Trucks

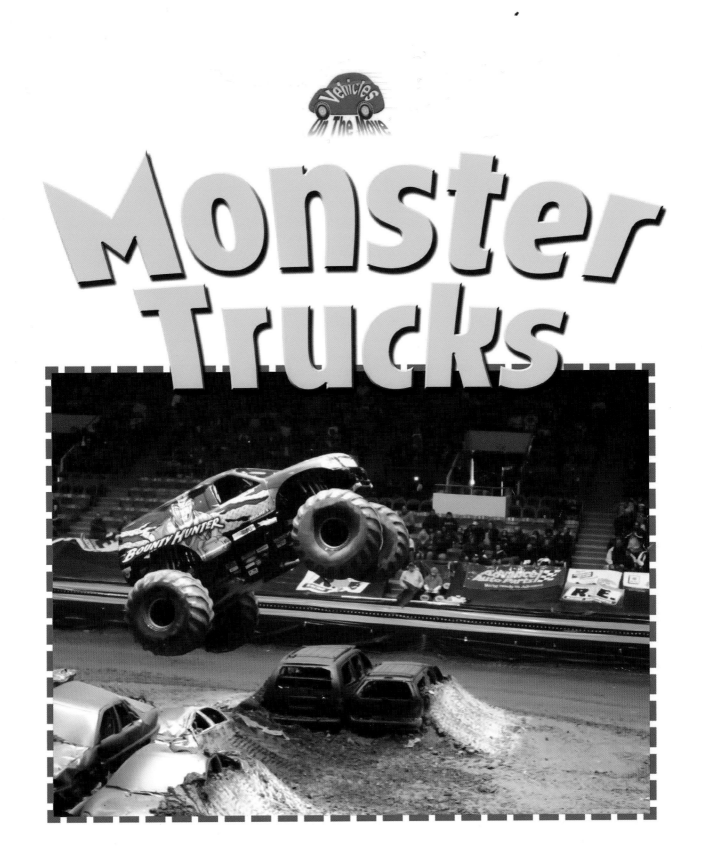

Lynn Peppas
🌳 Crabtree Publishing Company
www.crabtreebooks.com

Created by Bobbie Kalman

Author
Lynn Peppas

**Publishing plan research
and development**
Sean Charlebois, Reagan Miller
Crabtree Publishing Company

Editorial director
Kathy Middleton

Editor
Molly Aloian

Proofreader
Crystal Sikkens

Photo research
Samara Parent

Design
Samara Parent

**Production coordinator
and prepress technician**
Samara Parent

Print coordinator
Katherine Berti

Photographs
© Michael Doolittle / Alamy: page 10
Dreamstime.com: pages 8, 26; © Celso Diniz: page 13;
    © Falun1: page 3; © Gorgios: page 23; © Serena Livingston:
    pages 18–19; © Susanne Neal: page 29 (top)
Shutterstock.com: page 14; PhotoStock10: front cover; Alex
    Melnick: back cover, pages 5, 28; Barry Salmons: pages 9,
    24–25, 31 (top); Christopher Halloran: page 12; Felix
    Mizioznikov: page 11; Kenneth Vincent Summers: page 27;
    Michael Stokes: pages 6–7, 20–21; Natursports: pages 4, 15;
    Walter G Arce: title page
Wikimedia Commons: Tammy Powers: pages 16-17,
    29 (bottom), 30, 31 (bottom); Seth Whales: page 22

Library and Archives Canada Cataloguing in Publication

Peppas, Lynn
    Monster trucks / Lynn Peppas.

(Vehicles on the move)
Includes index.
Issued also in electronic format.
ISBN 978-0-7787-3019-4 (bound).--ISBN 978-0-7787-3024-8 (pbk.)

    1. Monster trucks--Juvenile literature. I. Title. II. Series:
Vehicles on the move

TL230.15.P427 2012   j629.224   C2012-900894-X

Library of Congress Cataloging-in-Publication Data

Peppas, Lynn.
    Monster trucks / Lynn Peppas.
        p. cm. -- (Vehicles on the move)
    Includes index.
    Audience: Grades K-3.
    ISBN 978-0-7787-3019-4 (library binding : alk. paper) -- ISBN 978-0-
7787-3024-8 (pbk. : alk. paper) -- ISBN 978-1-4271-7943-2 (electronic
pdf) -- ISBN 978-1-4271-8058-2 (electronic html)
    1. Monster trucks--Juvenile literature. I. Title.

TL230.15.P46 2012
629.223'2--dc23

                                                    2012004063

Crabtree Publishing Company

www.crabtreebooks.com   1-800-387-7650

Printed in the U.S.A./092014/CG20140808

**Published in Canada
Crabtree Publishing**
616 Welland Ave.
St. Catharines, Ontario
L2M 5V6

**Published in the United States
Crabtree Publishing**
PMB 59051
350 Fifth Avenue, 59th Floor
New York, New York 10118

**Published in the United Kingdom
Crabtree Publishing**
Maritime House
Basin Road North, Hove
BN41 1WR

**Published in Australia
Crabtree Publishing**
3 Charles Street
Coburg North
VIC 3058

Contents

What are Monster Trucks?

A monster truck is a vehicle with giant wheels. A vehicle is a machine that carries people from one place to another. A monster truck has a body that looks like a pickup truck. A pickup truck has an open **bed** in the back of the vehicle.

Monster trucks weigh about 10,000 pounds (4,536 kilograms). They cost about $250,000 to build.

A monster truck is big and powerful. They are fun vehicles to watch. They jump over and crush other vehicles such as old cars and buses. They show off their power in front of large crowds. They **compete** against other monster trucks.

frame

shocks

cab

MONSTERTRUXWALES.COM

LUCAS
OIL PRODUCTS
INC

DR

Parts of a Monster Truck

Monster trucks are **custom** made. Even though they look like pickup trucks, all their parts are giant-sized and specially made. A number of mechanics work together to build heavy-duty parts that do not break easily. Mechanics are people who build and fix vehicles.

body

shocks

engine

wheels

In the Driver's Seat

A monster truck driver sits in the cab of the truck. Monster trucks do not have doors. Instead, the driver climbs in through the window of the truck.

Drivers sit in the middle of the truck so they are better protected if the truck rolls over.

The floor of the cab has see-through panels. This helps the driver see where he or she is going when doing a wheelie. A wheelie is when the driver drives on the back two wheels only.

Drivers can see through a special window in the floor of the monster truck when they can't see out the front window.

Safety First

A monster truck is a very dangerous vehicle to drive. It crashes often and rolls over on its sides or roof. The driver must be strapped in with a seatbelt called a **harness**. It has more straps than a seatbelt in a car. The driver also wears a helmet and a **fireproof** suit.

A fireproof suit helps to protect the driver from getting burned if the truck catches fire.

A driver of a monster truck has a team of crew members that help him or her during a competition. If the driver has an accident, he or she shuts the truck off right away. If the driver cannot do it, a crew member can use a switch at the back of the truck or a **remote control** to turn the truck off.

Rescue crew members rush to see if the driver is okay.

Body Work

A monster truck's body, or outer shell, is made of fiberglass. Fiberglass is a **lightweight** material made of glass and plastic mixed together. It can be easily molded into different shapes. Some monster trucks are made to look like large pickup trucks, and others are shaped to look like animals or other vehicles.

A number of monster trucks have been created to look like dogs, such as this one named Brutus.

Every monster truck has a special name and paint job. It costs about $50,000 to design the first monster truck body. Monster truck bodies are often destroyed while performing. It costs about $3,000 to buy a brand new body that looks exactly the same.

Big Wheels

Monster trucks stand about 11 feet (3.4 meters) tall. They drive on huge tires that are almost 6 feet (1.8 meters) tall and 43 inches (109 centimeters) wide. These large tires help monster trucks move over different surfaces easily.

Monster truck tires are also used on large tractors.

Monster truck tires have deep treads. Treads are deep rubber grooves on the surface of the tire. Deep treads help the truck grip the ground. They stop it from slipping and sliding.

One monster truck tire costs about $1800.

Strong Frame

Monster trucks often roll over during **competitions**. For this reason they have heavy-duty frames. A frame is the vehicle's skeleton. Monster truck frames are specially made for monster trucks only.

The frame makes the vehicle sturdy and strong. The frame is made from steel tubes or pipes. They are round and hollow in the middle. Frames like these protect the driver from getting crushed. The frame also protects the engine and other truck parts inside.

The floor of the frame is called the chassis. The roll cage protects the driver inside the cab of the monster truck.

roll cage

chassis

Monster Engine

Monster trucks need monster engines to move their monster wheels. An engine is the machine that makes the monster truck move. Horsepower measures how much power a vehicle has. A monster truck engine has about 1700 horsepower. Heavy-duty pickup trucks only have about 400 horsepower.

Monster truck engines cost about $35,000. One truck uses up to five engines in one year. Monster truck engines run on a **fuel** called methanol. Racecar engines also use methanol fuel. It takes about 8 gallons (30 liters) of fuel to drive a monster truck one mile (1.6 kilometers).

engine

First Monster Truck

The very first monster truck ever made is called Bigfoot. It was built by Bob Chandler in 1975. It was made from the body of a Ford 250 pickup truck. In 1981, Bigfoot drove over some junkyard cars and crushed them. People loved watching it.

Bigfoot began crushing cars during other vehicle competitions. Bob and his team started to build more monster trucks in the 1980s. The trucks grew to be bigger and stronger. He named many of them Bigfoot.

Bigfoot, the monster truck that began it all, is still going strong today!

Monster Truck Tracks

Monster trucks cannot drive on roads or highways. They are specially made to compete at monster truck events. These are held in outdoor or indoor stadiums. A stadium has a large, **oval** track that is surrounded by rows of seats.

Some monster truck shows have specially made dirt tracks for the vehicles to drive on. It takes a crew of eight people about three days to build the track. The track often has ramps on one side for the monster trucks to race and an open area on the other for them to perform **stunts**.

Junkyard cars—sometimes even motor homes—are brought into the stadium for the trucks to drive over.

Monster Truck Racing

Monster trucks compete against each other during monster truck races. On some racecourses, there are ramps for the trucks to jump over. Other racecourses have piles of junk cars, buses, motor homes, or even small planes for the trucks to climb over and crush.

Drag racing is an event where vehicles race at top speed in a straight line for a short distance. Monster trucks drag race against each other for the best time through an obstacle course. An obstacle is something that is in the way.

Most monster trucks can drive up to 80 miles per hour (129 km/h).

Freestyle

Freestyle is an event where stunts and style matter more than speed. Monster truck drivers perform stunts to show off their driving **skills** or to impress the audience. Sometimes there are competitions where drivers get points for doing stunts. The truck with the most points wins the competition.

Spinning the vehicle around in a circle is called a donut.

One monster truck stunt is called a slap wheelie. A slap wheelie is when a monster truck jumps over an obstacle and bounces when it lands. This is the slap. Then the driver drives the truck up on its back two wheels only and drives forward.

Famous Mon-star Trucks

One of the most **popular** monster trucks is called Grave Digger. It has a spooky graveyard picture painted on the body with a skull and a haunted house. It has glowing red headlights, too. There are more than 20 monster trucks made that are called Grave Digger.

Grave Digger is a favorite with fans at monster truck competitions across the United States.

Monster truck fans also like watching El Toro Loco, which means "the Crazy Bull" in Spanish. Another crowd favorite is Maximum Destruction. Maximum Destruction was the first monster truck to do a backflip.

You win some and you lose some. El Toro Loco wins the race and Maximum Destruction loses a wheel.

More Famous Mon-star Trucks

Monster truck owners give their monster trucks special names. They make them fun to look at with special paint jobs and shapes. Jurassic Attack is a monster truck with painted scales, horns, and a head frill that makes it look like a triceratops dinosaur.

A monster truck called Samson has two muscular arms on the sides of the truck body. Monster Mutt is a truck painted like the head of a dog. It has ears that hang over the sides and a tongue that sticks out of the front of the vehicle.

Fun truck designs make monster trucks even more fun to watch.

Glossary

bed The flat floor at the back of a truck

compete To go against others to win a game or competition

competition An event or game where people compete against each other to win

custom To make or build something the way a buyer wants

fireproof Something that will not catch on fire

fuel A material that is burned to provide power

harness Straps or belts that hold something in one place

lightweight Something that is not very heavy or does not weigh a lot

oval A shape that is long and round at the ends

popular Very well liked

remote control A switch that can be used from a distance away

shocks An object on a vehicle that acts like a spring and helps give a smoother ride

skill The ability to do something

stunts Special tricks

Index